CLARE MARIE

Divine Mercy Novena

Copyright © 2025 by Clare Marie

All rights reserved. No part of this publication may be reproduced, stored or transmitted in any form or by any means, electronic, mechanical, photocopying, recording, scanning, or otherwise without written permission from the publisher. It is illegal to copy this book, post it to a website, or distribute it by any other means without permission.

First edition

This book was professionally typeset on Reedsy.
Find out more at reedsy.com

Contents

Table of Content	1
Introduction	3
Day 1 – For All Mankind, Especially Sinners	7
Day 2 – For Priests and Religious	8
Day 3 – For All Devout and Faithful Souls	9
Day 4 – For Those Who Do Not Believe in God and Those Who Do...	10
Day 5 – For the Souls of the Separated Brethren	12
Day 6 – For the Meek and Humble Souls and the Souls of...	14
Day 7 – For Those Who Venerate and Glorify God's Mercy	16
Day 8 – For the Souls in Purgatory	18
Day 9 – For Lukewarm Souls	20
Additional Prayers and Devotions	22
Conclusion	24

Table of Content

Introduction

Novena to Divine Mercy

(Each day includes reflections, prayers, and intentions as revealed by Jesus to St. Faustina.)

Day 1 – For All Mankind, Especially Sinners
Day 2 – For Priests and Religious
Day 3 – For All Devout and Faithful Souls
Day 4 – For Those Who Do Not Believe in God and Those Who Do Not Yet Know Jesus
Day 5 – For the Souls of the Separated Brethren
Day 6 – For the Meek and Humble Souls and the Souls of Little Children
Day 7 – For Those Who Venerate and Glorify God's Mercy
Day 8 – For the Souls in Purgatory
Day 9 – For Lukewarm Souls

Additional Prayers and Devotions

Conclusion

Introduction

What is Divine Mercy?

Divine Mercy is the infinite and unfathomable love and compassion of God towards humanity, particularly sinners. It is the very essence of God's relationship with His people—a mercy that forgives, heals, and restores. This devotion is rooted in Scripture, as seen in the Psalms:

> "Give thanks to the Lord, for He is good; His mercy endures forever."
> *(Psalm 136:1)*

Jesus Himself repeatedly emphasized His mercy, especially in His public ministry. He healed the sick, forgave sinners, and welcomed the lost. The greatest act of mercy was His Passion, Death, and Resurrection, through which He opened the doors of salvation for all.

The Divine Mercy devotion calls us to trust in God's mercy, extend mercy to others, and pray for the conversion of sinners. It is a spiritual refuge for all souls, offering hope in the face of sin, suffering, and despair.

The Message and Devotion of Divine Mercy

The Divine Mercy message is simple but profound: **God's mercy is available to everyone, and He longs for souls to trust in Him.** Jesus revealed to St. Faustina Kowalska, a Polish nun, that His mercy was the last hope for humanity.

The devotion consists of several key elements:

1. **The Divine Mercy Image** – A painting of Jesus with rays of red and white light emanating from His Heart, symbolizing the blood and water that flowed from His side on the Cross. The image includes the words, **"Jesus, I trust in You."**
2. **The Chaplet of Divine Mercy** – A powerful prayer given to St. Faustina, which is prayed on a rosary and calls upon God's mercy for the whole world.
3. **The Hour of Mercy (3 PM Prayer)** – A special time of prayer at 3 PM, remembering the moment of Jesus' death and calling upon His mercy.
4. **The Feast of Divine Mercy** – Celebrated on the Sunday after Easter, this feast was established by St. John Paul II as a day of extraordinary grace and forgiveness.
5. **The Divine Mercy Novena** – A nine-day prayer dictated by Jesus to St. Faustina, bringing different groups of souls to His mercy each day.

The Divine Mercy devotion is not just about prayers but also about a way of life—showing mercy to others through acts of love, forgiveness, and compassion.

The Role of St. Faustina Kowalska

St. Maria Faustina Kowalska (1905–1938) was a humble Polish nun who received mystical revelations from Jesus. She recorded these divine encounters in her diary, *Divine Mercy in My Soul*, which became the foundation for the Divine Mercy devotion.

INTRODUCTION

Jesus called her to be the **"Apostle of Divine Mercy"** and entrusted her with the mission of spreading His message of love and forgiveness. She endured suffering, misunderstandings, and physical illness but remained faithful to her calling. Her diary contains messages from Jesus, emphasizing the urgency of trusting in His mercy.

Some of the most powerful words spoken by Jesus to St. Faustina include:

"The greater the sinner, the greater the right he has to My mercy." (*Diary, 723*)

"Mankind will not have peace until it turns to the fount of My mercy." (*Diary, 300*)

St. Faustina was canonized by Pope St. John Paul II in 2000, and the Divine Mercy devotion became officially recognized by the Church.

The Divine Mercy Chaplet and Novena

The **Divine Mercy Chaplet** was given to St. Faustina as a prayer for obtaining God's mercy, not only for ourselves but for the whole world. It is a simple yet powerful prayer that invokes God's mercy upon humanity, especially for sinners and the dying.

The **Divine Mercy Novena** was dictated by Jesus to St. Faustina in 1937. It consists of nine days of prayer, beginning on **Good Friday** and leading up to **Divine Mercy Sunday** (the first Sunday after Easter). Each day, Jesus asks for prayers for different groups of people, including sinners, priests, religious, and even those who are lukewarm in faith.

The novena is a journey of intercession, bringing souls into the ocean of God's mercy. Jesus promised that through this novena, He would grant special graces, especially to those who trust in His mercy.

How to Pray the Novena

The Divine Mercy Novena is prayed using the following structure:

1. Begin with the **Sign of the Cross**.
2. Say the **Opening Prayer** of the novena for the specific day.
3. Pray the **Divine Mercy Chaplet**, using a standard rosary.
4. Conclude with the **Closing Prayer** and the invocation:
5. "**Jesus, I trust in You.**"

It is most powerful when prayed at **3 PM**, the Hour of Mercy, as Jesus encouraged. However, it can be prayed at any time of the day.

Why Pray the Divine Mercy Novena?

This novena is a profound way to experience God's mercy in our lives. Some of the key reasons to pray it include:

- **For the forgiveness of sins** – Jesus promised that His mercy is greater than any sin.
- **For conversion and healing** – Praying for others, especially those far from God, brings them closer to His grace.
- **For peace and trust** – The novena helps deepen our trust in God's perfect plan, even amid suffering.
- **For the dying and souls in purgatory** – Jesus emphasized the power of this prayer for souls at the hour of death.
- **For the grace of Divine Mercy Sunday** – Jesus promised extraordinary graces to those who participate in this devotion, including a complete renewal of their souls.

As we embark on this novena, let us open our hearts to Jesus' mercy, trusting that no matter how great our weaknesses or failures, His love is greater.

Day 1 – For All Mankind, Especially Sinners

"Today bring to Me all mankind, especially all sinners, and immerse them in the ocean of My mercy."

Reflection

On the first day of the novena, Jesus invites us to bring all of humanity before Him, with a special focus on sinners. His heart burns with love for those who are far from Him, and He longs to shower them with His mercy. No sin is too great for His forgiveness, and He desires that all souls turn to Him in trust.

Prayer

Most Merciful Jesus, whose very nature is to have compassion on us and to forgive us, do not look upon our sins but upon our trust in Your infinite goodness. Receive all mankind into the abode of Your Most Compassionate Heart, and do not refuse anyone Your mercy. May all people come to know the greatness of Your mercy and glorify it forever.

Divine Mercy Chaplet (Pray the chaplet as instructed.)

Day 2 – For Priests and Religious

"Today bring to Me the souls of priests and religious, and immerse them in My unfathomable mercy."

Reflection

On this day, Jesus asks us to pray for priests and religious—those whom He has called to be His instruments of grace in the world. They are entrusted with leading souls to God, administering the sacraments, and living lives of holiness. Yet, they too face struggles, weaknesses, and temptations. Our prayers help sustain them in their mission.

Prayer

Most Merciful Jesus, from whom all good comes, we ask You to pour out Your grace upon priests and religious, who are called to reflect Your love and mercy. Strengthen them in their vocation, fill them with zeal for souls, and protect them from all evil. May their words and actions lead many to trust in Your mercy.

Divine Mercy Chaplet

Day 3 – For All Devout and Faithful Souls

"Today bring to Me all devout and faithful souls, and immerse them in the ocean of My mercy."

Reflection

Faithful souls strive to live according to God's will, yet they too need His grace to persevere. Jesus loves them deeply and desires to pour out even greater blessings upon them. He calls them to be beacons of light, spreading the message of Divine Mercy to others.

Prayer

Most Merciful Jesus, You never reject those who seek You with sincere hearts. We bring before You all devout and faithful souls who long to grow in love for You. Strengthen their faith, deepen their trust, and fill them with Your grace so that they may be witnesses of Your mercy in the world.

Divine Mercy Chaplet

Day 4 – For Those Who Do Not Believe in God and Those Who Do Not Yet Know Jesus

Jesus' Words to St. Faustina

"Today bring to Me those who do not believe in God and those who do not yet know Me. I was thinking also of them during My bitter Passion, and their future zeal comforted My Heart. Immerse them in the ocean of My mercy." (Diary, 1216)

Reflection

On this day of the novena, Jesus calls us to intercede for those who have not yet come to know Him—atheists, agnostics, and those who, through no fault of their own, have not yet encountered the Gospel. He reminds us that even as He suffered on the Cross, He had these souls in His heart, longing for the day they would find Him.

The world today is filled with those who search for meaning but do not know where to turn. Some reject God due to past hurts, others have been led astray by false teachings, and still, others have never had the opportunity to hear the truth of Christ. This day is a powerful moment to pray for their conversion, trusting in the boundless mercy of Jesus.

"I am the way, and the truth, and the life. No one comes to the Father except through me." *(John 14:6)*

DAY 4 – FOR THOSE WHO DO NOT BELIEVE IN GOD AND THOSE WHO DO...

Prayer

Most Merciful Jesus, You are the light of the world. We bring before You those who do not yet know You and those who reject You. Draw them to Yourself with the power of Your love. Remove the blindness from their eyes, soften their hearts, and let them recognize You as the source of truth and peace. May they one day share in the joy of eternal life with You.

Pray the Divine Mercy Chaplet

Day 5 – For the Souls of the Separated Brethren

Jesus' Words to St. Faustina

"Today bring to Me the souls of those who have separated themselves from My Church and immerse them in the ocean of My mercy. During My bitter Passion they tore at My Body and Heart, that is, My Church. As they return to unity with the Church, My wounds heal, and in this way, they alleviate My Passion." (Diary, 1218)

Reflection

On this day, Jesus asks us to pray for our separated brethren—those who have fallen away from the Catholic Church and those in other Christian traditions. He grieves over division, for the Church is His Mystical Body, meant to be one.

Throughout history, divisions have arisen, leading to different denominations and misunderstandings. Many have left the faith due to personal hurts, confusion, or lack of understanding. Yet, Jesus desires that all Christians be united in one flock under one Shepherd.

As we pray for unity, we also ask for humility in our own hearts. True unity will not come through argument or force but through love, prayer, and the witness of holiness.

DAY 5 – FOR THE SOULS OF THE SEPARATED BRETHREN

"I pray that they may all be one, as You, Father, are in Me and I in You." *(John 17:21)*

Prayer

Most Merciful Jesus, You are the Good Shepherd who seeks out the lost and brings them home. We lift up to You all who have separated themselves from the fullness of Your Church. Pour out Your grace upon them, heal wounds of division, and lead them back to the unity You so deeply desire. May we all be one, as You and the Father are one.

Pray the Divine Mercy Chaplet

Day 6 – For the Meek and Humble Souls and the Souls of Little Children

Jesus' Words to St. Faustina

"Today bring to Me the meek and humble souls and the souls of little children and immerse them in My mercy. These souls most closely resemble My Heart; they strengthened Me during My bitter agony. I saw them as earthly Angels, who would keep vigil at My altars. I pour out upon them whole torrents of grace. Only the humble soul is able to receive My grace; I favor humble souls with My confidence." (Diary, 1220)

Reflection

The Kingdom of Heaven belongs to the meek, the humble, and the pure-hearted. On this day, Jesus calls us to pray for those who have embraced simplicity, trust, and humility—especially children and those who live with childlike faith.

Children are a special gift in the eyes of God. They trust fully, love purely, and rely on their caregivers completely. This is the type of faith Jesus calls us to have—a heart that trusts completely in the Father's providence.

In a world that values power, status, and self-reliance, humility is often overlooked. Yet, God resists the proud and gives grace to the humble. Today, we pray for those who have remained meek in heart, as well as for ourselves, asking for the grace to embrace humility.

DAY 6 – FOR THE MEEK AND HUMBLE SOULS AND THE SOULS OF...

"Whoever humbles himself like this child is the greatest in the kingdom of heaven." *(Matthew 18:4)*

Prayer

Most Merciful Jesus, You rejoice in the pure of heart. We bring before You the meek, the humble, and the innocent—especially little children. Pour out upon them the abundance of Your grace. Keep them close to Your Sacred Heart, protect them from sin, and let them always remain in Your love. Give us, too, the grace to become like little children, trusting in You with simplicity and faith.

Day 7 – For Those Who Venerate and Glorify God's Mercy

Jesus' Words to St. Faustina

"Today bring to Me the souls who especially venerate and glorify My mercy, and immerse them in My mercy. These souls sorrowed most over My Passion and entered most deeply into My Spirit. They are living images of My Compassionate Heart. These souls will shine with a special brightness in the next life. Not one of them will go into the fire of hell. I shall particularly defend each one of them at the hour of death." (Diary, 1224)

Reflection

On this day, Jesus calls us to pray for those who dedicate themselves to spreading, living, and glorifying His Divine Mercy. These souls understand the depths of His love and reflect it in their lives. Whether through prayer, works of charity, or proclaiming the message of mercy, they console His Heart.

To venerate and glorify Divine Mercy means more than just reciting prayers—it is a way of life. It is choosing to forgive when it is difficult, showing kindness to the undeserving, and trusting in God's will even in suffering. The promise that Jesus makes to these souls is extraordinary: He will defend them at the hour of death and they will not suffer condemnation.

As we pray today, let us ask for the grace to be counted among those who

DAY 7 – FOR THOSE WHO VENERATE AND GLORIFY GOD'S MERCY

glorify God's mercy, living it out in our daily lives.

"Blessed are the merciful, for they shall obtain mercy." *(Matthew 5:7)*

Prayer

Most Merciful Jesus, You have promised special protection to those who venerate and spread the message of Your Divine Mercy. Look with love upon these souls who trust in You completely. Strengthen them in their mission, increase their love for You, and help them to be living witnesses of Your mercy in the world. May we, too, glorify Your mercy in word and deed, and may we trust in You always.

Pray the Divine Mercy Chaplet

Day 8 – For the Souls in Purgatory

Jesus' Words to St. Faustina
"Today bring to Me the souls who are in the prison of Purgatory, and immerse them in the abyss of My mercy. Let the torrents of My Blood cool down their scorching flames. All these souls are greatly loved by Me. They are making retribution to My justice. It is in Your power to bring them relief. Draw all the indulgences from the treasury of My Church and offer them on their behalf. Oh, if you only knew the torments they suffer, you would continually offer for them the alms of the spirit and pay off their debt to My justice!" (Diary, 1226)

Reflection

On this day, Jesus invites us to pray for the souls in Purgatory, those who have died in God's grace but still need purification before entering heaven. They long to be with God, but their souls must first be cleansed of any remaining attachment to sin.

Purgatory is an expression of God's mercy, allowing souls to be purified so they can stand before His holiness. Yet, these souls can no longer pray for themselves—they rely on the prayers of the faithful, especially the offering of Masses and indulgences.

Jesus tells us that we can bring relief to these souls by offering sacrifices, prayers, and acts of mercy on their behalf. Let us commit ourselves to praying for them regularly, knowing that one day, they will intercede for us when they enter the fullness of God's presence.

DAY 8 – FOR THE SOULS IN PURGATORY

"It is therefore a holy and wholesome thought to pray for the dead, that they may be loosed from sins." *(2 Maccabees 12:46)*

Prayer

Most Merciful Jesus, You love all souls, and we bring before You those in Purgatory, who long for the day they will see You face to face. Pour out upon them the cleansing power of Your mercy, and hasten the time of their entrance into heaven. May our prayers and sacrifices be a source of consolation for them. Eternal rest grant unto them, O Lord, and let perpetual light shine upon them. May they rest in peace.

Pray the Divine Mercy Chaplet

Day 9 – For Lukewarm Souls

Jesus' Words to St. Faustina
"Today bring to Me souls who have become lukewarm and immerse them in the abyss of My mercy. These souls wound My Heart most painfully. My soul suffered the most dreadful loathing in the Garden of Olives because of lukewarm souls. They were the reason I cried out: 'Father, take this cup away from Me, if it be Your will.' For them, the last hope of salvation is to run to My mercy." (Diary, 1228)

Reflection
The final day of the novena is dedicated to the most heartbreaking group of souls—those who are lukewarm in faith. These souls neither reject nor fully embrace God's love; they live with indifference toward Him.

Jesus reveals that these souls caused Him the greatest agony during His Passion. Their lack of love, their complacency, and their neglect of His grace deeply wound His Heart. Yet, He does not abandon them—He calls them to awaken and seek His mercy before it is too late.

Lukewarmness is a dangerous spiritual state because it numbs the soul to God's presence. It makes one blind to sin, unconcerned with eternity, and resistant to conversion. Jesus urges us to pray fervently for these souls, that they may be set on fire with love for Him once more.

"I know your works; you are neither cold nor hot. Would that you were cold or hot! So, because you are lukewarm, and neither hot

DAY 9 – FOR LUKEWARM SOULS

nor cold, I will spit you out of my mouth." *(Revelation 3:15-16)*

Prayer

Most Merciful Jesus, today we bring to You souls who have become lukewarm in their faith. They neither reject nor embrace You fully, and their indifference pains Your Heart. Pour out upon them the fire of Your love, stir their hearts to conversion, and draw them back to a fervent life of faith. May they come to know the joy of surrendering fully to You.

Pray the Divine Mercy Chaplet

Additional Prayers and Devotions

While the **Divine Mercy Novena** is a powerful devotion on its own, many faithful find it helpful to incorporate additional prayers and devotions that deepen their relationship with God's mercy. Below are some recommended prayers and spiritual practices to accompany the novena.

The Divine Mercy Chaplet

The Divine Mercy Chaplet is a central part of this devotion. It was revealed to St. Faustina by Jesus as a way to offer God's mercy to the world. It is traditionally prayed using a rosary and includes the following prayers:

Opening Prayer (Optional)

"You expired, Jesus, but the source of life gushed forth for souls, and the ocean of mercy opened up for the whole world. O Fount of Life, unfathomable Divine Mercy, envelop the whole world and empty Yourself out upon us." (Diary, 1319)

On the Our Father beads:

"Eternal Father, I offer You the Body and Blood, Soul and Divinity of Your dearly beloved Son, Our Lord Jesus Christ, in atonement for our sins and those of the whole world."

On the Hail Mary beads (10 times):

"For the sake of His sorrowful Passion, have mercy on us and on the whole world."

Concluding Prayer (3 times):

"Holy God, Holy Mighty One, Holy Immortal One, have mercy on us and on the

whole world."

Act of Consecration to Divine Mercy

O Merciful Jesus, Your goodness is infinite, and Your mercy is without end. I consecrate myself entirely to You, trusting in Your unfathomable love. I desire to live my life in complete dependence on Your mercy, seeking refuge in Your Sacred Heart.

Help me to be merciful as You are merciful, to forgive as You forgive, and to love as You love. Let my words, actions, and thoughts reflect Your compassion. Jesus, I trust in You! Amen.

Prayer for Trust in Divine Mercy

Jesus, I trust in You. When I am weary and burdened, when I am afraid and uncertain, when I feel lost and alone, I trust in You. In moments of suffering, in times of temptation, in seasons of doubt, I trust in You.

You are my refuge, my strength, and my salvation. Help me to always rely on Your mercy and to extend that mercy to others. Jesus, I trust in You! Amen.

The Hour of Mercy (3:00 PM Devotion)

Jesus instructed St. Faustina to pray at **3:00 PM**, the hour of His death, as a moment of special grace:

"At three o'clock, implore My mercy, especially for sinners; and, if only for a brief moment, immerse yourself in My Passion, particularly in My abandonment at the moment of agony. This is the hour of great mercy for the whole world." (Diary, 1320)

At this time, one can pray:

- The **Divine Mercy Chaplet**
- The **Prayer for Mercy** (*"O Blood and Water, which gushed forth from the Heart of Jesus as a fount of mercy for us, I trust in You!"*)
- A moment of silent reflection on Christ's Passion

Conclusion

The **Divine Mercy Novena** is not just a devotion—it is an invitation to a deeper understanding of God's infinite love. By praying for different groups of souls, we join Jesus in His mission of saving and sanctifying the world. This novena reminds us that **no soul is beyond the reach of God's mercy**, and that by trusting in Him, we find true peace.

As we conclude, let us commit to living the message of Divine Mercy every day:

- **Trust in God's mercy** in all circumstances.
- **Show mercy** to others through our words, deeds, and prayers.
- **Spread the message** of Divine Mercy to those in need of hope and healing.

May the words of St. Faustina inspire us:

"Let no soul fear to draw near to Me, even though its sins be as scarlet. My mercy is greater than your sins and those of the entire world." (Diary, 699)

Jesus, I trust in You!

Made in the USA
Columbia, SC
10 July 2025